MW00876189

i'm
dealing
with
it

kaylee frazier

I'M DEALING WITH IT

Copyright © 2024 Kaylee Frazier

All rights reserved. No part of this publication may be reproduced, stored in a retrieval system, distributed or transmitted in any form or by any means – electronic, mechanical, photocopying, and recording or otherwise – without prior written permission from the author, except in the case of brief quotations in book reviews and other noncommercial uses permitted by copyright law. If you would like to use material from the book (other than for review purposes), prior written permission must be obtained by contacting the author.

Thank you for your support of the author's rights.

ISBN: 979-8-328-8349-7-1

Layout Design by: Rein G.
@reindrawthings (www.fiverr.com)

TRIGGER WARNING

This poetry book contains topics that may be troubling to some readers. Content is including but not limited to body dysmorphia, dysfunctional family dynamics, childhood trauma, abuse, foul language, and grief. Provided below are resources.

SAMSHA 1800-662-4357

988 Suicide and Crisis Lifeline

DEDICATION

First and most importantly, I want to say thank you to my incredibly supportive husband Clint. I'm sorry that the only thing that comes out when I write about you is the fact that you're a ginger. Even though you make it hard to relate to Taylor Swift songs now because you are a perfect partner, I love you dearly and you are the best thing that has ever happened to my Instagram messages. The next thank you goes to the ladies. Asha, Natalie, and Bridget, I can't put into words (even though I should be able to because I wrote this entire thing) how much I appreciate you pressuring me into chasing this dream and for the countless time you put into reading all my sad emo poems. I also can't not mention Ali, Lei, and Hai for simply always being there. Paula and Andrea, you two were the dream team. It was so much fun bringing this project to life and I adore you both.

Lastly, a shout out to every boy who broke my heart. This is how I'm dealing with it so thanks for making me a writer.

CONTENTS

where it all went wrong

They say the most important years of your life
are from three to five
That's when you're developing your idea
of self if you're wondering why
This shows you I was doomed from the start
And you could say my parents played
a very big part

Other kids said
There is a monster under their bed
But for me there is a monster running my house
He even has his very own spouse
He told me to call him dad
This monster is so very mad
I tried turning on all of the lights
But this one doesn't just come out at night
I promise you this isn't a lie
Can someone please help me I don't want to die
Don't leave me alone with this beast
I'm just a child to say the least

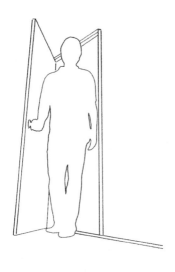

I was a part of you for nine months
Even shared the same guts
So how can you hate me

The first time it happened I ran and cried
The second time I wanted to die
The third time I told myself I deserved it
The fourth time my little sister observed it
The fifth time I zoned out
The sixth time I tried my best not to shout
The seventh time I fought back
The eighth time I knew better than that
The ninth time I mixed foundation in a cup
The tenth time I made a story up
Then I lost count

When I was ten, I'd sneak into my mom's room
I'd put on her clothes and spray her perfume
I'd do this every day until I got caught
Then she locked her door and told me to stop
Couldn't she see I just wanted to feel close
Maybe then I'd understand why
she disliked me the most

There's a worm in his brain I used to pretend
It's the only way I could comprehend
How one minute he'd be smiling and kind
Then the next he'd be screaming and losing his mind
He was always running hot then cold
The worm must have a mighty hold
Every now and then my dad would take back over
But the worm demanded all the exposure
It got to the point where he was gone for good
I'd never see him again that I understood

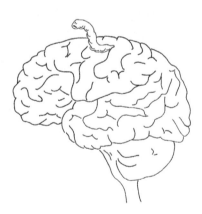

Roof over my head
Plenty of food to eat
So why do I feel so incomplete

There are holes in my memory
That no doctor can remedy
Places you should've been
Like when I was giving ballet a spin
Or on the day of my senior prom
Where all I wanted was my mom
Another was college graduation
I worked so damn hard for my education
Then when I said I do
To a man who has never met you
But deals with the damage you've done
These holes are all empty
Because you went and you left me

I hear a knock knock at the door
It's the emancipation I didn't ask for
Wasn't there something else we could do
Another idea we might pursue
You don't need to get rid of your kids
to get a new wife
We were once your favorite part of your life

Winter is creeping in lights are being hung
The holidays were only enjoyable when I was young
Now I don't have a house to fill with joy
My family has gone and gotten destroyed

You have abandonment issues
Here's a tissue
My therapist said
Walls up high
All those poor guys
My therapist said
Forgive your mom
She had a lot going on
My therapist said
Your dad's angry hands
Were fixed with name brands
My therapist said
There's really no need to be sad
I know so many who have it as bad
My therapist said
Depression is a choice
You just need to find your voice
My therapist said
Your time has ended
Another session is recommended
My therapist said

My escape became my prison
It wasn't like this before
But no one noticed I was getting called into
your office more
I'd try to make up a reason to stay far away
But I'd still have to face my captor every day
The walls were so high there was no getting out
A shell of myself I just moped about
This beautiful field I once cherished
Is now the very location I perished

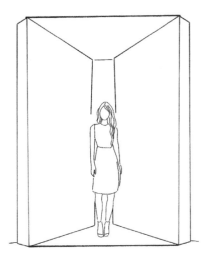

I wanted to take back a part that he stole
So I searched for something in my life
just I could control

I viewed eating as a game
How long can I go until I cave
Am I strong enough to last an entire day?

I work out to pass time
So, I can win this challenge of mine

My face is pale
Tik tok
My brain is hazy
Tik tok

Its 8pm and I get in bed
Another day of victory I said
As I shut my eyes the hunger finally subsides
Until I must rise again

Tearing myself down

Never enough

When will I ever stop being so rough

Oh, the poor girl in the mirror

Why won't I feed her

She is so broken

She is so sad

She thinks starving herself isn't that bad

Slowly withering away

Praying for the day

I love myself

Every therapist I've ever been to says I need to do shadow work but what do you do when your world is so dark shadows don't exist

I had to get to know me
You might ask how this could be
I am my least favorite person you see

I buried the pain of my childhood so deep
I didn't cry not even weep
I glued this smile on my face
Be pretty be smart or you're out of place
Don't let them know you're defective
No one must know not even a detective

I wrote this fake version of myself
To not deal with what I left on the shelf
It sits there covered in dust
Waiting patiently to be discussed

But I'm too scared to set it free
I don't want to deal with that part of me
If I keep the book closed
My life I can mold
I can keep playing pretend
Write my own pretty end

But if I open that book and go to that chapter
I know it will make me a damn disaster
I'm just not strong enough to deal
With all this pain and hurt I have sealed

Dear future baby
From the moment you are born
I promise I will pour
All the love I have to give
I'll feed you your bottles
And tighten you in your swaddles
So you can grow big and strong

I'll teach you to be kind
And how to use your mind
You can be whatever you want to be

I'll be there every step of the way
In my heart you will always stay
I am breaking the cycle

I always look like I'm walking on shells

It's because my childhood still dwells

I'd wake up each morning not knowing

who I'd get

Was It the man I looked up to or a threat

From smiling to frowning in the same
conversation

Not knowing what caused his sudden agitation

Each step I take is to prepare

You never know when you must beware

Am I bipolar

Or depressed

Someone put a title on this mess

At least if it has a name

I have somewhere else to point the blame

I tried to take some medication
That seems to be the answer for our generation
If you're sad, mad, or depressed
They've got a pill for you to digest
Does no one wonder why we are all this way
Is it because none of our parents' marriages
are okay
Over half of us are children of divorce
Yet a magic prescription is the only answer
they endorse

Society says
You must be pretty
You must be smart
Shoulders back
Play your part

Shave your legs
Lower your voice
Or you will be his second choice

Clean the house
Cook the food
Have a baby or two

Dream big
But just in your sleep
Your life is his to keep

looking for love
in all the wrong places

The drunkest I've ever been was the night we met
Even though water was the only drink I would get
My vision went blurry my cheeks were flushed
This had to be more than just a little crush
My knees were wobbly my hands shaking
I knew my heart was something you'd be taking
To feel this way forever was something I craved
But drinking too much can put you in a grave

A way to explain my boyfriend I desperately sought
Perhaps the loud screech of a tea pot
One second still- the next screaming high pitch
Reminds me of how fast he could switch
It never took long to get him to boil
Causing happy moments to quickly spoil
But after the steam was released from his spout
A beautiful cup of tea would come out

You've made your point
I always disappoint
I wore a bikini in April
It was too much of a staple
How dare I show my body off
Attention seeking slut you scoffed
I am to be for your eyes only
I know I'm losing myself slowly
But I put back on my cover up dress
Because I love you nevertheless

You can run out the door and be free
Scream that you regret me
You can speed and screech the tires on your car
But we both know you won't get very far
I'll wait for you in the driveway to admit defeat
Then we'll go and mess up the silk sheet
I love knowing that you'll always return
A healthy relationship is something
we will never learn

You said you loved my strong opinion
My fiery heart
My fierce decisions
But now you ask me to keep my mouth quiet
Stand behind you and stay silent
The girl you once adored was shoved into a box
Forced to reshape into something she's not
Did you ever really love those things about me
Or did you just like the idea of clipping my wings

How does it feel to tame the beast

Have her on the tightest leash

Show her off to all your friends

Knowing this is where her story ends

Are you proud you took the sparkle from her eyes

As she now hangs on your mantle like a prize

Was it something I said

Was it something I did

How we ended I don't even know where to begin

One moment we were perfectly fine

Now you're sitting here telling me not to cry

I'm gasping for air; it's all been taken away

How do I get up when I can't even feel my legs

My heads gone light

My jaws on the floor

I got blind-sided

As you slammed the door

I gave you so much of me
That now I am empty

I've never felt pain like this
Its running through my toes to my wrists
This is all so unfair
I'm reaching for a hand that used to be there
This bathroom floor is so damn cold
I never thought you'd let us fold
I haven't been able to eat in four days
I keep checking my phone to see if you wish
you'd stay
When you loved me, I believed it to be true
But now I'm curled up picturing you
with someone new

You said you didn't mind that I had no fame
No one out there ever knew my name
I'd wait patiently to the side as you'd greet
And take pictures of you with fans on the street
Brought you peace in the chaos that was your life
I guess that's why I'm surprised my back now
has a knife

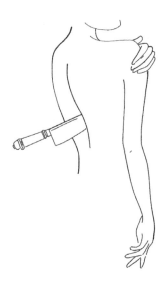

There's no way you're gone for real
Without you I don't know how to heal
You made your point now come back
If I'm left alone too long, I'll crack

Time keeps on moving
But all of this is so confusing
My body still won't stop shaking
My heart is brutally aching
I'm disappearing just skin and bones
Your name is still not popping up on my phone
Forever is what you always said
No one taught me how to mourn someone
who isn't dead

Growing up in the desert I thought
I'd be prepared for a drought
But being without you for this long
has me in doubt
I'm dancing for rain and praying to the sky
How many days without water will you let go by
Everything is withering and wilting away
I don't think I can last another day

Was I really just some object
The new star in your research project
Collecting data about how much one could take
Until they give up or snap and break
You never really loved me that'd be a contradiction
Tell me did I last longer than your prediction

You killed me
Figuratively
The girl I was once before
Now looks like she went through a three-year war
Came back with no medals to show for her time
And out of my grave I'll never be able to climb
While you carry on with the rest of your life

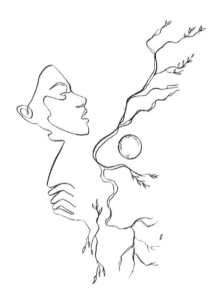

I loved you so much that I lost me
I gave up everything I wanted to be
I sacrificed it all in your name
You swore you wouldn't let it get to you, the fame
I spent all my money on flights
Cheered for you under the lights
Your name became so well known
That you started to hide your phone
You said it was you not me
You didn't understand ME had become WE
There was no individual left standing here
All of me had disappeared

I'm still on fire

From you being such a liar

My burns run deep

Tell me is the match something you still keep

I can patch the holes in the wall
Fix the stairs so we don't fall
I'll reupholster that couch you hate
Replace the old latch on the gate
I'll repaint the inside a nice shade of gray
If I redo our house, will you want to stay

My god fate is so cruel
Putting me here in the same bar as you
Timing is treacherous as we make eye contact
And before I know it we're in an uber
heading back
Three months of trying to heal all out the door
Your lips on my lips begging me for more
Does this mean you might actually miss me too
Is If you let it go and it comes back really true

I thought if we had one more night
Your feelings for me would reignite
But all that did was confirm you have all the power
Now I'm trying to scrub off my shame in the shower

I woke up to you hungover and naked
in my room
Telling me this was a mistake and we were
still through

You made sure you took from me one more time
I can assure you this will be your final crime

A part of me has finally hardened
Don't bother asking if you can be pardoned

I'll never be yours or anyone's again
You can keep your apology we can't be friends

You viewed our relationship as commensal
But you used a sharpie and I used a pencil
Your mark on me is still here to show
While you wiped mine away a while ago
Parasitism is a better definition
I was your host, and you took without my permission

The first time we were supposed to meet
my flight got cancelled
I should've taken that as a sign
But instead, I paid $600 to get the next one in line

I drove 4 hours after I landed
If you were creepy I would've been stranded

But that wasn't the case, you were cute and kind
Looking back, I understand now how I was
so blind

You liked to read books and were shy
I really thought I had a nice guy

You sent me flowers and wrote me notes
I started to believe in stupid love quotes

But as time went by you transformed
Maybe it was because on a bigger stage
you performed

You'll never step up and admit to cheating
But I have screenshots you thought were deleted

Now I wish I didn't get on that plane
It would've saved me a whole lot of pain

Now I think everything is a sign

From the outside looking in I was healing
But the truth is I have no idea what I'm even
feeling

I can't drive past Thomas Street
A part of me is left in your sheets

It's where I sat on the counter and told you
I loved you
Its where we'd make-out until our lips turned blue

We planned our entire lives there together
In your arms I thought I would stay forever

But now Thomas Street holds nothing but
memories
Like when I thought I was your bride to be

But my finger is now cold and bare
And all I can do is stare
As I take the long way home

Not even in my dreams can I escape your face
I'm forced to recall all I must try to replace

Do you miss me I whispered to the cracks
in the floor
It's nothing this house hasn't heard before
I resist the need to text you again
Knowing good and well our relationship is dead

I always hated Trader Joes
But I know it's a place you always go
So I'll buy groceries I don't need
Because it gives me a chance to be seen
I imagine we bump our carts
Or you see me from a distance
and the feelings restart
You'll say wow I didn't expect to see you here
How long has it been almost a year
You'll compliment me and ask me how I've been
I'll tell some lies and a great life I'll spin
You have so much fun catching up
That you ask to see me again and I can't
believe my luck
Next in line I hear someone say
And just like that out of my daydream
I'm ripped away

She asked me if I could be anyone in the world
who would I be
I said that's easy me at twenty-three
Riding in your jeep with the breeze flowing
through my hair
Running stop signs because you couldn't help
but stare
Refusing to drop me off until you get
one more kiss
You being that in love with me is something
I'll never not miss

Seasons change and so does the weather
Just last April we were together
Now it's November and I'm cold and alone
Teeth chattering as the wind is being blown
The only thing that has remained the same
Is you refusing to take any of the blame

I guess I'm just a little confused
Why am I the girl whose heart is bruised
And she's the one who gets you

It'll always be us why can't you see
Even Across the country you can't escape me
No matter how the clock ticks on
Or how many girls you try to con
You'll never reach the high we got together
Our souls undeniably tethered
The fighting and screaming and slamming of doors
The clothes thrown all over the floors
You can try to find it with someone new
But what you feel for them will never subdue
Because it'll always be me for you

The first date I went on after you
I sat in my car and cried to nothing new

With mascara running down my face
I stepped into what used to be our place

Except it wasn't you who was sitting
on the other side of the booth
It was a stranger and yes,
he was tall and cute if you want the truth

But there's not a human on this earth
that's a big enough distraction
To stop my brain from only thinking about
your reaction

None of his jokes were funny and he didn't
order dessert
He didn't have a freckle or chest hair fighting
to escape his shirt

He walked me to the car, told me he had a great
time and leaned in for a kiss
And for the first time in three years,
it wasn't your lips

My phone buzzed and it wasn't your name
It was him asking me on another date

You're a splinter in my mind I can't seem to get
Every time I try the deeper it's kept

Maybe you're not at all who I thought
Seeing who you ended up with has me distraught
She's tall and blonde and likes beer
I'm short and brunette and cry lots of tears
She's a modern-day beauty queen
I read books, write poems, and drink caffeine
I can't imagine what you even talk about
I feel like she's only dating you for clout
Don't you miss our deep 2am conversations
Or all my complex complications
Don't get me wrong I knew you'd move on
to someone new
I just never thought it'd be someone the opposite
of you

It was supposed to be me in white
Now instead of standing on the other side
of the alter saying I do
I'm on my phone to get a view
Of the man I once knew

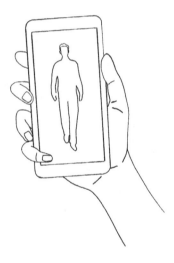

I had to fight the urge to send you
a Taylor Swift song
It reminded me of all that you did wrong
But I hit delete on the text
Because if you replied it'd leave me perplexed
So I'll just sit here and cry on my own
And be the saddest girl you've ever known

I saw her tik tok the other day
Bragging about the career she gave away
Stay at home wife who follows you around
Yet when we were together,
we couldn't even live in the same town
You said you only like girls who are
independent and humble
But without your money that relationship
would crumble
I loved you before all of the fame
I know she would've looked the other way
So did you lie to me about your type
Or have you changed so much that so did
what you like

I'm going on dates knowing I'm a dead-end street
It doesn't matter how many great guys I meet
If they're not you I simply have to profess
That they must have entered the wrong address

I batted my lashes and made deep conversation
We talked about his parents and my great education
I had him hanging on every word
Made him think he was who I preferred
I smiled and laughed at all his jokes
I truly am the greatest hoax

Bodies with faces
Things and places
The joy is only temporary
Then I'm back in the cemetery
Grieving for someone who still has breath
Even though he's alive I've had to put him to rest

I've only read books about the wild wild west
As a newly single girl I was just doing my best
I thought Texas was filled with faithful
Christian boys
Now I'm learning that's only a part of their ploy
Pulling you in with their scripture tattoos
Just to add you to their long queue
Most of them don't even live on a farm
But oh, let me tell you about their southern charm
They'll fill you with all you want to hear
Get your hopes up only to cheat then disappear

How toxic am I that I miss yelling and fighting
That shit was so damn exciting
Will you come back from slamming the door
Or will I go for days ignored
It was intoxicating the push and pull
The drama made me feel full
Now I'm with a man who doesn't raise his voice
Let's me know breaking up is never a choice
And it's all healthy and fine
But I miss walking that line
With you

Why are you so fucked in the head
You screamed at me as I cried in bed
You let what happened to you as a child
Create all these thoughts that are wild
I can't keep watching you self-implode
And being left to pick up the pieces
from your latest episode
I'm dealing with it I said under my breath
But it was too late you had already left

My taste in men was constantly in doubt
I always wondered why things never worked out
It wasn't until someone asked me about my dad
That it hit me harder than anything ever had
Was my problem with men my own fault
Because I didn't deal with what I kept in my vault

found.

My body was a weapon
My face was a trap
You knew the game I was playing yet
your hand is on my lap
My eyes say things my lips don't mean
But all you can see is the girl of your dreams
So you'll play by my rules if it gets you
even an hour
Tell me now was it worth it now that your heart
has been devoured

When I met you I was starving
I fed off your fear of losing me
Engorged in your apologies
Licked my lips clean
Knowing you'd never be able to leave
This is what love is I believed

The round and round
Pulling you in then cutting you down
Backing you into a corner with the webs
of gaslighting I spun
All this passion and drama made
the relationship fun

Until one night I overate
You looked into my eyes with so much hate
For the first time you pulled out your fork
and knife
Took such a big piece of me it ended my life

It's easy to sit here and point fingers
Hurt people hurt people
Go figure

I'm sorry you had that version of me
I was the villain in your story

I shouldn't have done what I did
I put so much pressure on you it blew the lid
You were my sole source of love
Now I see that's why we came undone
It wasn't your responsibility
To mend the broken pieces of me
You tried your best to hold me together
But no tape or glue would ever weather
The storm that is me

In the end I was just too much
I sucked the life out of you
And held it in my clutch
Just know that I'll always regret
Not getting the help I knew I needed to get
You'll forever have a piece of my heart
The hero in my story I Impart

Looking for love in all the wrong places

After it ends, I'm back off to the races

Searching high and searching low

Going any speed but slow

Offering my heart to strangers on the street

Doing whatever it takes to feel complete

Leaving myself no time to heal

Always onto the next one so I could feel

It wasn't until I was finally alone

That I found love was something I could

get on my own

How could he love someone who
has been undiscovered
You can't worry about anyone else until
you're fully recovered

I'm here looking in the mirror
I don't understand why you didn't see her
You took and took and took
I gave you all of me you crook
But now I'm standing on my own
Trying to put back together what you stole
I am more than a book on your god damn shelf
I belong only to myself

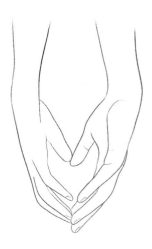

A person who requires no validation
Has control of every situation

On a beach in Greece with ABBA playing
I realized what all the self-help books were saying
I don't need a man by my side
Just an Aperol spritz, my girls, and the tide

I'm trying to heal my inner child
The things that were done to me were ever so vile
To survive I simply blacked everything out
This caused me to walk a very dark route
Now I'm back with a candle lighting the path
Trying to decrease the after math

I always thought I needed an apology
But words are just words you see
In the silence I healed me

There was a time I felt I had to make up lies
Embellish myself to be a prize
I'd play and act out all different parts
Whatever I had to do to collect hearts
I starred in these roles for oh so long
I couldn't even tell this version of me was wrong
Until one day I took a good long look in the mirror
Went to therapy and it all became clearer
I am not the things that have been done
I am in fact a one of one

I burned all the scripts and took off the mask
Now I am just me whenever anyone asks

Diving into your blue eyes

I'm drowning

Gulping water, you have me surrounded

But consuming you isn't stinging my lungs

I can still open my eyes and see above

Did I mix up the end with the beginning

That explains how I am now swimming

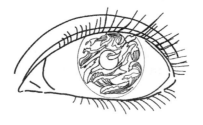

To you I wasn't a project or something to win
You simply wanted to see what was within
So I poured out all of my darkness
Told you of my upbringing and all of its harshness
I expected you to turn and run
But you grabbed my hands and out came the sun

I found out what cheating was when I was ten
My dad told me he was just playing pretend
But I heard my mom crying in her room
Screaming about another woman's perfume
I found out what abandonment was when
I was in my teens
My mom packed up all her things unseen
Her closet was emptied
No goodbye left for me
I found out what pain was at twenty-three
When he broke his promises to marry me
He said I was the one and we'd be together forever
Then moved onto someone better
I found out what love was at twenty-seven
He had red hair, blue eyes and was sent
straight from heaven
He didn't mind the baggage I carried around
In his freckled arms I was found

You have three loves in your lifetime
The first love will be fun and exciting
The second one will make you
feel like you're dying
But the third one will be slow
Comfortable and make you grow
It'll almost feel too easy
Makes you become super cheesy
Like your souls were made from the same pieces
His love for you never decreases
Not even on your very worst day
Will you question if he will stay
Now when I see the number three
I think about how life brought you to me

Our past is somewhere in the water
It's been many years since you took me
to the slaughter
I don't harbor as much anger anymore
I find I am much happier on the shore

I was covered in sharp points
Anywhere you'd touched me I'd disappoint
So many men tried to shave them down
With one prick of blood they'd turn around
But you asked me about every jagged edge
You weren't scared of scars you pledged
A cut can heal in four to six weeks
And you had all the healing techniques
One by one my thorns came off
Left with bright red petals I am now soft

I never thought I'd envy freckles
Little orange and brown speckles

A masterpiece swirled on your arms
You have no idea of their charm

A cluster around your bright blue eyes
These damn dots will be my demise

I'm jealous they get to touch every part of you
But wow what a fantastic little view

The loud honking of taxi cars

Floral pink dresses under the stars

I hated crowds and busy streets

Flashing lights and hotel suites

But in this city our love story would start

And because of that New York will always

have my heart

When I see orange, I see you
A color that is liked by only a few
Before I saw in black and white
Never anything so bright
Then my world got painted orange
Freckles and cats
So many laughs
Now my favorite color is orange

I was not looking for you
No way I was ready for someone new
I thought maybe we could be just friends
You told me that was not what you intend
You flew five plus hours
To the desert flowers
You were sweating from the heat
I thought your nerves were really sweet
We spent six days together
It wasn't enough however
You invited me to fly back to your state
I agreed because who am I to go against fate
I packed for only three days
Having no idea, I'd end up there to stay
Now I have a ring

I haven't even opened the menu yet
Before walking through the door,
you know what I'll get
There's nobody that understands me
quite like you
Together forever, we said I do
Love at first sight that's no exaggeration
I'll love you the rest of my days with no hesitation

You hate your crooked smile
Your unstraight teeth
You have to look beyond that
and see what's beneath
Your humor is endless
Your hearts as big as Mars
If only you could see yourself from afar
In my eyes you're perfect I wouldn't change
a thing
I smile every time I see you wearing your ring

That was their first-time living life as well
I explained to the little girl who went
through hell
It might not seem like it but maybe they were
doing their best
That doesn't make it right she stomped and
professed
Aren't you tired of being angry stuck
in the pitch black
I grabbed my inner child's hand,
and she grabbed back
It's time to move on and let it all go
This healed adult me she's happy to know

An ode to my 20s

My twenties were an absolute shit show.

I let a 40-year-old man convince me
I'd play better if I didn't eat
I lost my entire identity when I took off my cleats

I was so burdened from not dealing with
my childhood trauma
In order to feel loved there'd have to be drama

I cried on my bathroom floor for days
Because the guy I gave all of me to said
his feelings had changed

I went to therapy and she told me to cut
out the bad
That meant I had to walk away from my dad

I went out and made a lot of mistakes
Put my trust in people who ended up
being snakes

I lost myself more times than I can count
But I think I finally figured it out

I found me in the flowers that continued
to bloom
Even after enduring all the rain and gloom

I found me in women who never left my side
Picked me up whenever I'd cry

I found me in the calmness my husband brings
It really is the little things

I found me in all of this crazy mess
And because of this my 30s will be the best

I always thought it would be cool to date a writer
In order to meet deadlines, they'd pull an all nighter
But I married someone who only writes his name
So a poet I became
This way the stories of us can live on forever
Whichever "us" even the ones I severed

Now it's all out there in your hands you hold
The story of me I have finally told

ABOUT THE AUTHOR

Kaylee Frazier is an Arizona girl who now resides in Georgia with her husband and an embarrassing number of cats. In her spare time she likes to read, cook, binge watch reality tv, and go to pilates. She has loved books for as long as she can remember and crushed all the other kids in AR reading.

Stuck in the same endless pattern of destruction she realized she had a lot of work and healing to do. Her therapist recommended writing. *I'm Dealing With It* started as basic diary entries and blossomed into her reflecting on all the deepest darkest corners of her life through poetry.

She hopes in some small way this will help others feel like they aren't alone, and that life indeed does get better.

CONNECT WITH KAYLEE

Instagram: kayleefraz

TikTok: kayleefraz

X: kayleeefrazier

Made in the USA
Las Vegas, NV
09 November 2024

11438392R00066